Also by M J Harper

The History of Britain Revealed
(USA title: The Secret History of the English Language)

The Megalithic Empire (with H L Vered)

Meetings with Remarkable Forgeries

An Unreliable History of the Second World War

Revisionist Historiography

YouTube

A New Model of the Solar System
www.youtube.com/watch?v=uPWH9xh_Jy0

The Distribution of Deserts
www.youtube.com/watch?app=desktop&v=5uNQIMcKNTM

A Megalithic Trade Route
www.youtube.com/watch?v=VO6TFjNBJmU

Websites

The Applied Epistemology Library
www.applied-epistemology.com

The Megalithic Empire
www.themegalithicempire.com/forum/

Talking to Myself and Others

M J Harper

Applied Epistemology Library
publishing@aelibrary.co.uk

Contents

Family Life

Child: I can't stand it.

Parent: What now?

Child: Everything.

Parent: You've got very little to complain about.

Child: I've got everything to complain about.

Me (to child)**:** I can send you an address if you like.

Child: I wish you would.

Parent: What address?

Me: For people who want to run away and join the circus.

Parent: And you're going to help her, are you?

Me: I always give them their home address.

Me: Where are you sending Jonathan?

Parent: We're not *sending* him anywhere, he'll be going to a local comprehensive.

Me: I admire your rectitude.

Parent: What do you mean?

Me: Comprehensives can be rough in this part of town.

Parent: We've applied for a place at this new charter school.

Me: What if he doesn't get in? They don't have selective entry, do they?

Parent: I leave these things to madam. She knows the ins and outs.

Family member: So we're all agreed, we'll go ahead with a weekly Zoom hook-up. How are we going to pay for it?
Me: The poorest member pays for the whole thing.
Family member: Tell us why, we know you're dying to.
Me: The overall sum is too small to worry about, so one of us can pay for everybody.
Family member: But why the poorest? Why not the richest?
Me: Do you know who that is?
Family member: No.
Me: Nobody does. But we know who the poorest is, me, and I don't mind paying.
Family member: Absurd. What I propose is for me to pay the initial amount, then I'll email everyone with my bank details and what each of you should contribute. Don't worry, I'll send out reminders to the laggards. I'll do the same every three months, we don't want to commit to an annual membership. If we need to adjust the amount in future, as people join in or fall out, I can let you all know and you can adjust your contribution accordingly. Agreed?
All: Agreed!
Me (thinks): A shame. I wanted to keep control.

Politics

Him: You're terribly right-wing.
Me: I hope not, right-wing people make me vomit.
Him: You're certainly not left-wing.
Me: Thank God for that, left-wing people make me vomit.
Him: Don't tell me, you're somewhere in the middle.
Me: And vomit out of both sides of my mouth? No thanks!

Me: Do you always vote for the same party?
Voter: I usually vote Labour, but I have voted Lib Dem. Even Welsh Nationalist once when I lived there. The Greens in local elections occasionally.
Me: But not for the Conservative Party?
Voter: I would never vote Tory.
Me: Can you say why not?
Voter: I believe in fairness. I don't like the rich getting richer and the poor getting poorer.
Me: Statistics seem to indicate there's not much in it. If there's any effect on equality, it's marginal.
Voter: Marginal is good enough for me.
Me: But does it outweigh, say, social policies?
Voter: Oh, the left is miles better across the board.
Me: Crime and punishment, immigration, race, that sort of thing?
Voter: They don't call the Tories the Nasty Party for nothing.
Me: And green issues?
Voter: Labour could do better in that department but the Tories don't seem to care about the environment at all.
Me: How about foreign policy?
Voter: I'm in favour of an ethical foreign policy and, let's face it, that means a left-wing foreign policy.
Me: Naturally you voted to stay in the EU.
Voter: I rest my case.
Me: Thank you for your help.

Me: Do you always vote for the same party?
Voter: I usually vote Conservative. Though once for the Lib Dems in a by-election. But I'm thinking about Reform next time.
Me: But not for the Labour Party?
Voter: I would never vote Labour.
Me: Can you say why not?
Voter: They just spend our taxes on harum-scarum schemes that never work.
Me: Statistics indicate there is little correlation in the level of taxation whoever's in power.
Voter: A little correlation goes a long way.
Me: But what about Labour's other policies? The NHS, public transport, the arts and so forth?
Voter: A little correlation doesn't go very far.
Me: Crime and punishment, immigration, race, that sort of thing?
Voter: Yes, they're soft on them as well.
Me: Green issues?
Voter: They all seem to be saying the same thing.
Me: Foreign policy?
Voter: They'd sell us out if they had their way.
Me: Did you vote to leave the EU?
Voter: In a heartbeat.
Me: Thank you for your help.

Him: Sorry, I can't agree with you there. I'm a socialist.
Me: I doubt it. Not a real socialist.
Him: Who are you to say what I am and what I'm not?
Me: I can tell by your clothes, your hairstyle and your glottal stops.
Him: You doubt my sincerity?
Me: I'm judging you by it. It oozes from every pore.
Him: So what does a *real* socialist look like?
Me: Since real socialism can only be achieved by chicanery and violence, I doubt that a real socialist would go round wearing sandals.
Him: I'm not wearing sandals.
Me: Metaphorically.

Me: Have you revised your opinion about Trump?

Him: No way, José.

Me: Even though he's ended six wars in six months.

Him: You believe that, you'll believe anything.

Me: You've checked, have you?

Him: No way, José.

Voter: I'm sorry but I think it's completely irresponsible.

Me: What, me not voting?

Voter: People died to...

Me: No, they didn't.

Voter: There was that suffragette...

Me: I already had the vote by then.

Direct Action

Me: How was the march?

Protestor: Inspiring. There were so many of us.

Me: Yes, it was on the news. Fifty thousand, they said.

Protestor: Oh, at least. That's a conservative estimate, I'd say.

Me: It was the estimate of the organisers. The police said twenty thousand.

Protestor: They would, wouldn't they?

Me: Why do you say that?

Protestor: It's routine. The police always downplay the numbers.

Me: It's certainly routine for the police to have to estimate the size of crowds—football supporters, Boxing Day shoppers, New Year celebrators, what have you.

Protestor: So?

Me: It's not a skill march organisers are likely to have.

Protestor: So you're just going to swallow the police estimate, are you?

Me: No, I was estimating how many police officers are involved in working out the number of marchers, deciding it was fifty thousand plus, then agreeing among themselves to put out a figure of twenty thousand.

Protestor: I certainly wouldn't put it past them.

Me: No, I suppose not. But then, as you say, it's routine. So you'd have to factor in all those people, working out the true figures of protest marches held everywhere in the world, for as long as anyone can remember and then lying about the true figure.

Protestor: The police are bastards. End of.

Me: I'm sure you're right. All the more reason to think one of them would have sold the story to the papers. A specialist misinformation unit in the local police force must be worth a bob or two to a tabloid. Nearer twenty grand than fifty though, I would have thought.

Me: Are you sure you ought to go?
Young Adult: We have to stop those fascist scum.
Me: But won't you be giving them the oxygen of publicity, there's so few of them.
Young Adult: It'll be the right kind of publicity when people see us turning out en masse to scatter them every which way except forward.
Me: They'll be protected by the police.
Young Adult: 'Nuff said.
Me: Well, don't get arrested.
Young Adult: I won't. I'm only small fry.
Me: Even so…
Young Adult: *Even so!* Look what happened in Germany when people did nothing.
Me: I thought the Nazis came to power because of street rioting between them and their opponents.
Young Adult: Don't wait up.

Couch potato: It's outrageous. All they want is to join the EU.
Me: No, they don't.
Couch potato: How can you say that? Read their placards.
Me: Oh, sure, the people on screen do, but they're hardly representative of the general population, are they?
Couch potato: How do you know that?
Me: They're wearing leather.
Couch potato: What's that got to do with anything?
Me: Only young, urban, dissident people wear leather.
Couch potato: *And* are the most likely to be out demonstrating in a repressive state with a government that is a Russian lapdog.
Me: True, but when you notice it, it can only mean they're the *only* people demonstrating. Yet we have the evidence on screen: anyone *could* be demonstrating if they wanted to. So it's safe to assume the general population isn't particularly bothered about joining the EU.
Couch potato: You do talk rubbish sometimes.
Me: You'd be saying similar things if they were protesting about too many immigrants.

Mental Health

Psychiatrist: Do you know why you're here?

Me: Because I'm the greatest brain in the known universe?

Psychiatrist: No, it's because you *say* you're the greatest brain in the known universe.

Me: Do you know why you're here?

Psychiatrist: I'm a consultant psychiatrist.

Me: No, it's because you *say* you're a consultant psychiatrist.

Psychiatrist: I think you'll find there are people who agree with me.

Me: I think you'll find there are people who agree with me.

Psychiatrist: I doubt that very much.

Me: Actually, you've got a point there. Not in so many words.

Psychiatrist: Words can be very important. Do you maintain, here and now, hand on heart, you are the greatest brain in the known universe?

Me: I do.

Psychiatrist: If I can persuade you that's an irrational statement, you'll be well on your way out of here.

Me: If I can persuade you it's a rational statement, will I be well on my way out of here?

Psychiatrist: I think that's enough for today. We can resume here in my office, tomorrow at two o'clock.

Psychiatrist: You were going to tell me your claim to be the greatest brain in the known universe is a rational statement.
Me: OK, but first do you understand the difference between a rational statement and a true one?
Psychiatrist: I think so. Is the distinction going to be important?
Me: Absolutely. I won't be able to demonstrate it is a true statement, only a rational one.
Psychiatrist: But surely you think it is a true statement.
Me: I do, otherwise I wouldn't be making it. But I do not anticipate being able to persuade you it is true, only rational.
Psychiatrist: Understood. Go on.
Me: The phrase 'in the known universe' means we are talking about human beings, would you accept that? We don't know of any other great brains, do we?
Psychiatrist: It's a strange way of putting it, but all right, yes.
Me: The 'greatest brain' a human being can possess must mean a brain that exists here and now, would you accept that?
Psychiatrist: No, I wouldn't. What about, say, Isaac Newton?
Me: He may have the finest brain but you yourself have a greater brain than his. You know everything he knew, he didn't know a fraction of what you know.
Psychiatrist: In that limited sense, yes, I agree.
Me: So to identify the greatest brain in the known universe means looking around for the smartest dude on the planet right now?
Psychiatrist: I think we'll leave it there, I'd like to consult some colleagues. Same time tomorrow.

Me: Are you the smartest psychiatrist on the planet?
Psychiatrist: I wouldn't have thought so.
Me: Name three practicing psychiatrists smarter than you.
Psychiatrist: I can name three who are more eminent.
Me: Answer the question.
Psychiatrist: Well, no, I suppose I can't.
Me: Can you name three psychiatrists who are less smart than you?
Psychiatrist: Plenty, but don't ask me to name them.
Me: How did you judge they were less smart than you?
Psychiatrist: I read their papers, I listened to them at case cons, I interviewed them for jobs...
Me: It wasn't difficult?
Psychiatrist: Well, I must stress it's all very subjective and I'm only referring to the... shall we say, more egregious examples.
Me: But if it was *every* psychiatrist you came across in a long and varied career, and if the gulf between you and them was a country mile, wouldn't you conclude you were the smartest psychiatrist on the planet?
Psychiatrist: No, I would conclude I was suffering from one or more of a variety of psychiatric disorders.
Me: Oh dear. Same time tomorrow?

Subjective Arguments

Art historian: Lovely painting, isn't it?

Me: Yes, it is.

Art historian: So very modern in its treatment.

Me: Of course it might *be* modern.

Art historian: Don't start on that again.

Me: It's not me saying it. They say between a third and a half of all paintings in public art galleries are fakes.

Art historian: Who are *they*?

Me: Oh, you know, experts.

Art historian: I thought you didn't trust experts.

Me: I do when they're making sense.

Art historian: And up to a half of everything here being fake makes sense, does it?

Me: I'd probably go for 'between a half and two-thirds'.

Art historian: How have you managed to work that out? Not being an art expert.

Me: By applying Gresham's Law. If genuine paintings are rare and expensive, they will be driven out by cheap and readily available substitutes.

Art historian: On that argument, everything here would be fake.

Me: I was going to say 'between two-thirds and three-thirds' but I didn't want to be accused of spreading alarm and despondency.

Art historian: That would be a first.

Economist: All signs say we're heading for a slump.
Me: How do you know?
Economist: It's called the 'business cycle'.
Me: There is no such thing as the 'business cycle'.
Economist: You've examined annual change in GNP over time?
Me: Since 1780, yes.
Economist: And what did you find?
Me: A bell curve centred on two per cent annual growth.
Economist: String them out on a timeline and you will see all the booms and busts since 1780. In other words, the business cycle.
Me: In other words, random variations in changes to annual GNP between 1780 and now. Nothing more.
Economist: Why don't we take a look then? There! Do the 1930's look random to you? Do the 1860's look random?
Me: Yes. They are chance sequences of negative numbers that are bound to occur occasionally in any random sequence of integers varying with decreasing probability the further they are from plus 2. The 1930's and 1860's are just unusual but inevitable clusters of down years over a span of hundreds of years.
Economist: In other words, slumps.
Me: Not in other words, they *were* slumps. The Great Depression and the Overend-Gurney Crisis respectively.
Economist: Preceded by the boom of the 1920's and followed by the boom of the 1940's. What's that if it isn't a cycle?
Me: It's not a cycle. Look at the actual numbers. Most of them are positive because the long-term trend is plus two. Virtually all years are positive. You're only calling these particular ones 'booms' because they're juxtaposed to an unusual run of negative figures.
Economist: It's a classic case of boom and bust.
Me: It's a classic case of people determined to impose patterns on a chaotic multicausal situation so they can kid themselves they have some control over it. Which is mostly a good thing.

Me: Neither Russia nor China can be dealt with in the ordinary way because they are not nation-states.

Strategy expert: What are they then?

Me: They are 'contiguous-territory empires'.

Strategy expert: What's the difference?

Me: An empire has uncertain boundaries and an indeterminate existence, a nation-state has fixed boundaries and is immortal.

Strategy expert: What total poppycock.

Me: Only because you've never thought about it before.

Strategy expert: For a start, China has had an existence longer than any other state in recorded history. I wouldn't call that 'indeterminate'.

Me: We don't know China's future, and its borders have been changing throughout its recorded history.

Strategy expert: We don't know the future of these 'nation-states' of yours, do we?

Me: Yes, we do. Or at least we have a historical record of a very large number of them and over a very long time, and they have all retained the same borders and they have all proved to be immortal.

Strategy expert: And how are you defining these 'nation-states' of yours?

Me: Our working definition is 'Any sovereign state that retains the same borders for the lifetime of its inhabitants'.

Strategy expert: Sounds a bit circular to me.

Me: It would be if there were not so many examples of the phenomenon and with no exceptions.

Strategy expert: Still sounds like poppycock, I'm afraid.

Me: That is always the case when experts are confronted with new ideas they don't wish to examine.

Strategy expert: I certainly won't be examining this one.

Me: According to Neo-Darwinist theory, all animals have evolved from other animals.
Biologist: Yes, so?
Me: So all animals must experience a period of time when they co-exist with the animal that gave rise to them.
Biologist: Yes, so?
Me: That period might be short, it might be indefinitely long.
Biologist: Yes, so?
Me: Therefore all animals can be divided into two categories: those whose ancestral animal is still around and those whose ancestral animal is extinct.
Biologist: Yes, so?
Me: Including right now.
Biologist: Yes, so?
Me: Leaving aside any animal that has a connection with human domestication, can you name an animal whose immediate ancestor is still around and the name of that ancestral animal?
Biologist: Not offhand, no. It's not something I've ever felt a pressing need to consider. I'll send you an email.
Me: I think you'll find you won't.

Me: According to linguistic theory, all languages have evolved from other languages.

Linguist: Yes, so?

Me: So all languages must experience a period of time when they co-exist with the language that gave rise to them.

Linguist: Yes, so?

Me: That period might be short, it might be indefinitely long.

Linguist: Yes, so?

Me: Therefore all languages can be divided into two categories: those whose ancestral language is still around and those whose ancestral language is extinct.

Linguist: Yes, so?

Me: Including right now.

Linguist: Yes, so?

Me: Leaving aside any language that has commercial, sacerdotal or artificial associations, can you name a language whose immediate ancestor is still around and the name of that ancestral language?

Linguist: Not offhand, no. It's not something I've ever felt a pressing need to consider. I'll send you an email.

Me: I think you'll find you won't.

Me: So where do we come from then? Originally.

Palaeoanthropologist: Africa.

Me: Oh yes, Out-of-Africa. I've heard of that.

Palaeoanthropologist: Do you have a problem with it?

Me: Not if there's good evidence.

Palaeoanthropologist: There is. It's overwhelming.

Me: Go on, overwhelm me.

Palaeoanthropologist: Mitochondrial DNA mutates at a constant rate and, since these changes can be counted in modern populations, it's possible to say how long the whole process took.

Me: And?

Palaeoanthropologist: African populations have the greatest number of mitochondrial mutations, hence they are the oldest.

Me: I thought we were all descended from the same, as it were, genetic Adam-and-Eve.

Palaeoanthropologist: We are.

Me: So everyone alive today must have the same length of genetic history, i.e. from 'Adam-and-Eve' until now.

Palaeoanthropologist: Um…

Me: If mitochondrial DNA mutates at a constant rate we will all have pretty much the same number.

Palaeoanthropologist: Um…

Me: So if we have different amounts of mitochondrial mutations, it must be down to some factor other than age.

Palaeoanthropologist: Um…

Me: So Out-of-Africa is a crock.

Palaeoanthropologist: There's other stuff.

Me: Such as?

Palaeoanthropologist: It's not my field, I'll send you an email.

Anthropologist: I'm an anthropologist for my sins.

Me: What's your particular specialty?

Anthropologist: I've written a few papers on early civilisations.

Me: Have you worked out how it got started? Civilisation, I mean.

Anthropologist: I don't know that it *has* started sometimes.

Me: But you know when and where, technically speaking.

Anthropologist: Oh, yes, that's nailed on. Fourth millennium. Sumer was the first cradle civilisation.

Me: Why Sumer?

Anthropologist: I don't know. I don't think anyone does.

Me: What's in Sumer?

Anthropologist: Desert, Tigris/Euphrates, that's about it.

Me: Are rivers in deserts common?

Anthropologist: Obviously not, but they do exist.

Me: Anything unusual about the Tigris and Euphrates?

Anthropologist: Like what?

Me: Two rivers running parallel for a thousand miles seems unusual.

Anthropologist: Can't say I've noticed.

Me: It's unique. What with river capture and so on.

Anthropologist: If you say so.

Me: What are the other cradle civilisations?

Anthropologist: In sequence and allowing for a bit of give and take, there's Egypt, the Indus Valley, North China and Mexico.

Me: All places where there are rivers in deserts.

Anthropologist: Are they? I've never really thought about it. Well, nice talking to you, would you like me to send you a book covering it all?

Me: Why do you think no archaeological evidence of an early medieval monastery has been found on Lindisfarne?

Archaeologist: On the contrary, it very much has.

Me: But nothing diagnostic of a monastery.

Archaeologist: Inferential. Strongly inferential. It's only a matter of time before we find the monastery building itself.

Me: How much time? There've been thirty-two excavations in the last twenty-five years.

Archaeologist: A monastery is a very contextualised site.

Me: Lindisfarne is a very small island.

Archaeologist: We know it's there because of the historical evidence.

Me: How many excavations will it take before you question the historical evidence?

Archaeologist: We do not, as a matter of academic convention, question another discipline's findings.

Me: When you're in someone else's hole, stop digging.

Me: Glastonbury Tor looks artificial to me.
Geologist: No, entirely natural. It's down to geology. The hill is made of harder rock and the softer rock surrounding it has eroded away over time, leaving the Tor standing out in the flat landscape.
Me: How can you tell all that?
Geologist: It's fairly obvious.
Me: Humour me, I'd like to know, not being a geologist.
Geologist: I couldn't say off hand in the case of the Tor, I'd have to consult the local geological surveys.
Me: I have. They make no mention of whether it is natural or artificial.
Geologist: They wouldn't. It's assumed to be natural.
Me: There's a branch of geology devoted to how you tell the difference?
Geologist: I shouldn't think so. I've never heard of one if there is. And why should there be? If it's man-made, it wouldn't fall under 'geology' anyway.
Me: No, but the difference is important for identifying megalithic monuments. Silbury Hill was just a hill until it was recognised as the biggest earthwork in Europe.
Geologist: That was a long time ago.
Me: You won't be able to assist me in the case of Glastonbury Tor then?
Geologist: I don't intend wasting my time confirming something that's obvious.

Me: Where does the term Middle Ages hail from?
ChatGPT: The term "Middle Ages" was coined by Italian humanists during the Renaissance, in the 15th and 16th centuries.
Me: And why on earth would they do that?
ChatGPT: They viewed this period as a "middle time" between the perceived greatness of classical antiquity and their own era, which they believed marked a rebirth of civilization.
Me: Ooh, get them. Cheeky mares. But do go on.
ChatGPT: Specifically, the Latin term "media tempestas" ("middle season") first appeared in 1469. Later, variants like "medium aevum" (first recorded in 1604) and "media saecula" (first recorded in 1625) emerged.
Me: Yes, yes, but when did it go mainstream?
ChatGPT: The historian Leonardo Bruni was the first to use a tripartite periodization (ancient, medieval, and modern) in his 1442 work, History of the Florentine People. This model became standard after the 17th-century German historian Christoph Cellarius also adopted this three-period division.
Me: No, I mean really mainstream. You know, in English.
ChatGPT: The term medium aevum in Latin was Anglicized as "middle ages" in 1618. The adjective "medieval" (or "mediaeval"), meaning pertaining to the Middle Ages came into wider use in the 19th century.
Me: So if the Middle Ages stretched all the way from Rome to the Renaissance, when the hell was the Dark Age?
ChatGPT: The Renaissance, often seen as a distinct period, actually overlapped with the Late Middle Ages (1300-1500), with some scholars like Petrarch contrasting the "light" of the Renaissance with the perceived "darkness" of the preceding centuries.
Me: Surely the Dark Ages didn't extend until 1300?
ChatGPT: The term "Dark Ages" is also associated with the Middle Ages, particularly the early part, but is now less frequently used due to its negative connotations.

Me: When was the 'Dark Age'?
Historian: We do not employ the term Dark Age. It would be considered a gross breach of correct terminology.
Me: Everyone else does.
Historian: What, in common parlance, might be referred to as the Dark Age is the Early Middle Age, an adjunct to the Late (sometimes 'High') Middle Age.
Me: So it wasn't 'dark'?
Historian: We deplore such vulgar generalisations, preferring to emphasise the continuity of history between the end of the Roman Empire in the West c 400 AD and the Renaissance c 1450 AD.
Me: What about the continuity of history between the Roman Empire and this Early Middle Age you speak of? There doesn't seem to be any.
Historian: I couldn't say, it's not my field. You would have to take the matter up with Early Medievalists and Classicists.
Me: I've tried. They don't seem to have much to say on the subject.
Historian: And what have you concluded from that?
Me: That the Early Medieval period is an artefact created by historians.

Philologist: The text is written in Old English.

Me: I'm not surprised, it was written a long time ago.

Philologist: No, I mean it's written in Anglo-Saxon.

Me: I thought you said it was written in Old English.

Philologist: Old English *is* Anglo-Saxon.

Me: I'm confused. If it's all one language, why have two names for it?

Philologist: It's just convention, I suppose.

Me: Is this convention applied to any other language?

Philologist: How do you mean?

Me: Well, do the French, for instance, refer to Latin as Old French?

Philologist: No, but then they couldn't because Latin became lots of different languages.

Me: Why didn't Anglo-Saxon?

Philologist: It just didn't.

Me: So is there any reason to suppose Anglo-Saxon became English?

Philologist: *Anglo-* equals *English*, the clue is in the name.

Me: You mean, like *Français* equals *Frankish*?

Philologist: No, that's different.

Me: Clearly.

Me: Did you know your country is disappearing?
Geographer: First I've heard of it.
Me: Where do you live?
Geographer: London.
Me: In the Thames Valley then?
Geographer: Last I heard.
Me: What's happening at the headwaters of the Thames?
Geographer: Another rock festival?
Me: It's cutting back constantly via erosion.
Geographer: So I am given to understand.
Me: Until when?
Geographer: You're going to tell me. I've got that feeling.
Me: It will break into the Severn Valley. The two drainage areas are already separated only by a sliver of high ground.
Geographer: That is inevitable.
Me: Either the Thames will capture the Severn or the Severn will capture the Thames.
Geographer: That's what it's called right enough.
Me: There will be water all the way from the Bristol Channel to the Thames Estuary.
Geographer: By definition.
Me: The Atlantic Ocean will have joined up with the North Sea.
Geographer: That's one way of putting it.
Me: Britain will be two completely separate islands.
Geographer: They'll still be British Isles though.

Me: Did you know your country is disappearing?

Geomorphologist: First I've heard of it.

Me: Where do you live?

Geomorphologist: London.

Me: In the Thames Valley then?

Geomorphologist: Last I heard.

Me: How old is the Thames Valley?

Geomorphologist: Say, twelve thousand years. Since the last Ice Age.

Me: What will happen to the Thames Valley eventually?

Geomorphologist: It will be turned into golf courses?

Me: Every time it rains, topsoil gets removed. This is washed off into a tributary of the Thames, makes its way along the river proper before eventually being deposited on a mudbank in the Thames estuary.

Geomorphologist: Reckon so.

Me: It's a one-way process. Nothing's coming back.

Geomorphologist: One day, all this will be mudflats.

Me: The mudflats will be eroding too every time it rains. One day, all this will be sea with mud just under the surface.

Geomorphologist: In the long run we're all dead.

Me: Not so long. If it only took ten thousand years to create the Thames Valley, we can be reasonably sure it will only take another ten thousand years to reach the mudflats-under-the-sea stage.

Geomorphologist: Plate tectonics will take care of it.

Me: The continents will be long gone before there's time for that.

Me: Have they nailed down the greenhouse effect being the cause of global warming?

Physicist: It's been unarguable science for thirty years.

Me: You know that isn't true.

Physicist: Well, unargued except by climate-change deniers.

Me: No, that it's science. One thing you can't do with the earth is run replicated blind trials.

Physicist: You misunderstand what science is. It can involve many techniques. Lab experiments, computer modelling, all sorts.

Me: I doubt they've even done that. It would be constantly featured on TV documentaries if it had.

Physicist: We know quite enough physics—and chemistry—to be confident. These are very basic processes.

Me: We know little about the basic processes of the upper atmosphere.

Physicist: Everyone professionally concerned is satisfied.

Me: But as you say, it's unargued.

Physicist: What's that supposed to mean?

Me: Nobody's been arguing about a theory to which some doubt must attach. That might have been fair enough when there were climate-deniers around, but it is unforgivable to be so complacent now.

Physicist: What exactly do you think we are being complacent about?

Me: Since it is the future of the human race, one would think a few resources might be devoted to explanations other than the greenhouse effect. Just in case.

Physicist: They probably are.

Me: We would have heard if they were.

Physicist: I wouldn't know, it's not my field.

Me: I do. It *is* my field.

Climatologist: Your theory depends on ocean water not evaporating.
Me: That's true.
Climatologist: I'm not going to entertain any theory that breaks the most elementary laws of physics.
Me: You're absolutely certain it breaks the laws of physics?
Climatologist: Of course I am. It can be demonstrated in the lab.
Me: Not on an oceanic scale.
Climatologist: It's the same principle.
Me: Lots of things change when they're scaled up.
Climatologist: I'm sure it's been measured at sea. I would have thought oceanographers have done it innumerable times.
Me: But you don't know whether they have or they haven't?
Climatologist: Obviously not. Why would I?
Me: And you don't intend to check?
Climatologist: You check, it's your theory.
Me: I have. They had to scale it up.

Crossing America

Me: Why are you driving at well over sixty when the speed limit is 55?
American: Nobody observes speed limits in the Land of the Free.
Me: But surely they make sense, if only to get everyone driving at the same speed?
American: True, but they're always being set lower, often a lot lower, than the speed people think reasonable.
Me: Like this road, for instance. Fifty-five does seem a bit daft.
American: That's why I'm doing sixty-five.
Me: What about being pulled over by the police?
American: If you're ten miles over, they don't bother. But I agree, you might be unlucky.
Me: Who decided on 55 in the first place?
American: Probably somebody figured out 55 maximized safety while guzzling the least gas.
Me: Except for the fact that everyone ignores it.
American: Yup.
Me: And nobody seems able to change it.
American: Nup.
Me: So, your policy on speed limits has produced an outcome that is not safe, is not green, doesn't produce either a uniform or an optimum speed, creates a constant fear of being stopped by the police who mostly don't thereby creating not only manifold individual opportunities for both unfairness and corruption but brings the whole fabric of law and order into disrepute. Everyone knows all this and nobody can do a blessèd thing about it. Except bitch.
American: Yup.
Me: That's one helluva country you've got.
American: Yup.

American: We're coming up to the Continental Divide.
Me: There isn't a continental divide in America.
American: Well, here's the sign. Read it and weep.
Me: It says 'Continental Divide'. Doesn't make it so.
American: Three hundred million people can't be wrong.
Me: What do *you* understand it means.
American: It means the rivers of the continental USA flow either into the Pacific Ocean or the Atlantic Ocean. Couldn't be simpler.
Me: So if I named a city in the continental USA, you'd be able to say which side of the divide it was on.
American: I might have to phone a friend but, yes.
Me: St Louis.
American: St Louis? It's on a tributary of the Mississippi, which flows into the Gulf of Mexico, part of the Atlantic Ocean, so St Louis is on the eastern side of the continental divide.
Me: Denver.
American: Denver, Colorado. So that's presumably on a tributary of the Colorado which flows into the Gulf of California, part of the Pacific Ocean, so it's on the western side of the divide.
Me: Salt Lake City?
American: I'd have to phone a friend on that one.
Me: No need, the clue is in the name. All its precipitation runs into the Great Salt Lake. None of the rivers in that part of the United States run into either the Pacific or the Atlantic Ocean.
American: I'll take your word for it.
Me: So which side of the continental divide is Salt Lake City on?
American: No side, I guess.
Me: So there isn't a continental divide in the USA, is there?
American: Sorry, but until they take the sign down I'm going with the flow.

American: Here we are, Los Angeles, home sweet home.
Me: Were you affected by those wildfires last year?
American: Some.
Me: And maybe next year by the sound of it.
American: My insurance has certainly gone through the roof.
Me: What's causing it all?
American: Everything's so dry. We've had a drought for years.
Me: How come?
American: Global warming apparently.
Me: Why should that cause droughts?
American: We chalk it up to El Niño.
Me: That can't be right. Isn't El Niño as regular as clockwork?
American: A combination of the two or something.
Me: So global warming *and* an El Niño produces a drought year.
American: Yes.
Me: And global warming and *no* El Niño produces a drought year?
American: Have you got a better idea?
Me: I wouldn't have mentioned it if I hadn't.

Reviews

TV exec: I loved your book. I'm sure we can work something out.
Me: The subject matter's a bit old hat for me. I'd much prefer working with you on my current project. I sent you a treatment.
TV exec: Yes, I read it with interest. But it was a bit off the wall, I'm afraid. Not for us.
Me: The book was off the wall.
TV exec: It certainly was, that was what got our attention.
Me: Surprising really, you guys not having a background in the field.
TV exec: You explained it so well.
Me: I used the same techniques in the treatment I sent you.
TV exec: Sorry, but we didn't think that one hung together at all.
Me: Still, that is strange.
TV exec: What is?
Me: You could see one worked and the other didn't even though you didn't know much about either. But me, after spending years mugging up on both, couldn't see it at all!
TV exec: Sorry, but you've got to go with your gut in this business. Another drink? It's my shout.
Me: I'll take a rain check. Things to do.

Book reviewer: This is a terrible book. You're such a bullshitter.
Me: And, it seems, a very bad one too.
Reviewer: What do you mean?
Me: Bullshitters try to hide the fact that they're bullshitting, you spotted me straight off.
Reviewer: If the shoe fits...
Me: It's much worse than that.
Reviewer: How do you mean?
Me: I've written an entire book on the subject, I really put some welly into it. Yet you spotted it was bullshit without breaking stride even though, I'm guessing, you don't know all that much about the subject.
Reviewer: No, but I review a lot of books.
Me: I *write* a lot of books but, obviously, not anymore. It'll be gut-wrenching having to give it all up. What the hell am I going to do now?
Reviewer: Don't upset yourself. Maybe I was a bit harsh. I'm sure there must be some good stuff in it.
Me: You mean you were bullshitting?

Opponent: You must be a Russian troll to write this bollocks.
Me: I can think of two more likely explanations.
Opponent: Like what?
Me: Maybe I don't know as much as you do about the Ukraine War.
Opponent: That's certainly true judging from your previous posts.
Me: Or maybe I'm just all round less smart than you are.
Opponent: That's certainly true.
Me: Correct me if I'm wrong but there would seem to be three possibilities. One, I could be ignorant about Ukraine. Two, I could be just plain stupid. Three, I'm a Russian troll.
Opponent: Or all the above.
Me: Not quite. You believe both one and two to be true, yet you have opted for the third despite not knowing whether it was true or not.
Opponent: Is this leading somewhere?
Me: Oh yes, you're going to be shown the door.
Opponent: How do you work that out?
Me: Acting as a Russian troll is a crime in this country. I'm pretty sure that unwarrantably accusing a fellow-member of criminal activity is against the rules of this forum. So, unless you apologise for calling me a Russian troll, here, in writing, in a sincere and heartfelt manner, I shall be making a formal request to the Site Administrators to have you ejected.

Big Fish (on Facebook)**:** Calling it a fake is just a conspiracy theory.
Me: I didn't call it a fake, I said a scientific test would ensure it wasn't.
Big Fish: Amounts to the same thing. You're ignoring the unanimous opinion of dozens of experts. Or maybe you're claiming to be an expert yourself.
Me: It doesn't require an expert to know that if dozens of experts come to a unanimous conclusion about something that is by definition arguable, something must be wrong.
Big Fish: And that's enough to question the bona fides of a much-loved national treasure, is it?
Me: If it's a much-loved national treasure, isn't it worth a five-minute, fifty-pound, non-destructive, scientific test?

Me: Hello, are you still there?

Best Behaviour

Animal lover: That's terrible news. They should do something about it.
Me: They say all the African big five are in danger.
Animal lover: Big five?
Me: Lions, rhino, buffalo, elephants, leopards.
Animal lover: If they can't do anything about it, perhaps *we* should.
Me: We can.
Animal lover: What?
Me: Experience has shown the best way to conserve these animals is to allow them to be trophy-hunted.
Animal lover: Killing them to keep them alive, is that it?
Me: Well, yes, it amounts to that. Ordinary game parks are no use, poaching is rife in all of them. Without any protection at all things are even worse.
Animal lover: I don't see what *we* can do about it. It has to be an African solution to an African problem.
Me: Trophy hunting is so popular with rich westerners that setting aside game parks for them is more profitable than either agriculture or tourism. The locals—both people and government—protect the animals very effectively. Trophy hunting in itself does not affect overall numbers.
Animal lover: If you say so. But like I say, what can *we* do?
Me: We could repeal the law we passed a few years ago banning the import of 'trophied' animals.
Animal lover: Yes, I remember that. It was after that American so-called big game hunter shot a lion in Zimbabwe that turned out to be a national treasure, wasn't it? There was a terrible hullabaloo.
Me: Especially from you, as I remember.

Citizen: Why are you throwing away all this bread?
Me: It's not fresh enough.
Citizen: But it's not stale either.
Me: Bread's so cheap you might as well eat fresh.
Citizen: That's not very green of you.
Me: On the contrary, I'm the greenest person I know.
Citizen: That's ridiculous. We throw hardly anything away.
Me: I practically live on bread. I couldn't do that unless the bread was outa sight.
Citizen: And that makes you green, does it?
Me: I've seen what you live on. The airmiles are outa sight.

Me: I'm opposed to statutory equal pay for men and women.
Woman: You would be, you're a man.
Me: How many men opposed to equal pay do you know?
Woman: None that I'm aware of.
Me: I'm the only one then?
Woman: Yes, so?
Me: In that case, it can't be because I'm a man.
Woman: So why *are* you opposed to equal pay?
Me: Basically, it's because I'm smarter than those men.
Woman: That's not difficult.
Me: And women.

Me: I'm opposed to multiculturalism.
Non-white person: You would be, you're white.
Me: How many white people opposed to multiculturalism do you know?
etc

Me: I'm opposed to egalitarianism.
Left-wing person: You would be, you're middle class.
etc

Me: I'm opposed to all -isms.
etc

Citizen: Are you an anti-Semite?

Me: I suppose I am, yes.

Citizen: You should be thoroughly ashamed of yourself then.

Me: It's the Jews that should be ashamed.

Citizen: Now you're just being flat-out racist.

Me: Me? I didn't decide to call my country 'the Jewish state'.

Citizen: Jews and Israelis are not the same thing.

Me: Jews either live in Israel or support Israel.

Citizen: Not all of them.

Me: Enough of them to make generalisations valid.

Citizen: It's still racist.

Me: Am I allowed to be, say, anti-Russian?

Citizen: They're not a race, are they?

Me: Nor are Jews.

Citizen: They are a religious and cultural group.

Me: Jewishness and Judaism is not the same thing.

Indian: No, I don't, I'm a Hindu.

Me: You believe in Ganesh, the Elephant God?

Indian: Well, that's more for children...

Me: So you don't believe in Ganesh, the Elephant God?

Indian: It's complicated.

Me: You either believe in Ganesh, the Elephant God, or you don't.

Indian: Are you some sort of racist?

Me: You're Welsh?

Welshman: And proud of it.

Me: Why?

Welshman: Where do I start?

Me: With Welsh would be a good place.

Welshman: How do you mean?

Me: When did it become a written language, for instance?

Welshman: Very early on, comparatively. Fifth, sixth, seventh century, thereabouts.

Me: You don't seem very sure.

Welshman: Well, not much survives from those times but certainly early Welsh appears, as marginalia, in gospel books of the seventh/eighth century.

Me: How do you know they're seventh/eighth century?

Welshman: I don't personally. But that's the unanimous view of scholars who are paid to know these things.

Me: Welsh scholars?

Welshman: They're the only ones who can read Welsh.

Citizen: It's not surprising. Look at the conditions they have to live in. There's rubbish everywhere.

Me: Whose fault is that?

Citizen: The government's. They're responsible for collecting it.

Me: It's the same government where I live and there isn't rubbish everywhere.

Citizen: You're white and middle class. The government cares more about you than it does about them.

Me: But it's the same story everywhere they live. You're not telling me every government wherever they live doesn't care about them.

Citizen: Well, it certainly isn't the Inuits' fault.

Me: The poor are not important.
Citizen: What a disgusting thing to say.
Me: I didn't say the poor are not important to me.
Citizen: Sounds like it.
Me: I mean the poor are not important to society.
Citizen: You're being disgusting again.
Me: No, descriptive. The poor are always marginal to society.
Citizen: They ought not to be.
Me: That's the problem.
Citizen: Glad to hear you say so.
Me: No, I don't mean the poor should not be marginal. They are, as a matter of definition.
Citizen: You're going to say 'The poor are always with us' next.
Me: They always have been, haven't they?
Citizen: So, what *is* the problem then? In your opinion.
Me: They are used by oppositional factions to pursue various objectives.
Citizen: Such as?
Me: To stop being the opposition and start being the government.

Me and My Friends

Me: Would you say we are roughly equal in terms of having the same basic facts, intelligence and general education?

Friend: I wonder sometimes but, yes, I suppose so.

Me: In that case, why do you think we're always disagreeing?

Friend: It's because you're a bit of a pratt. Sorry, but that's the way it seems to me. You're always saying such soppy things.

Me: You mean I'm constantly in error?

Friend: You seem perversely proud of it.

Me: Otherwise you would change your position, wouldn't you?

Friend: I haven't found it to be necessary thus far.

Me: So when you say *A* and I say *not-A*, either one of us might be right. It's fifty-fifty, all things being equal.

Friend: In theory.

Me: But of course we might both be wrong.

Friend: In theory.

Me: So, when it comes to theoretical proposition *A,* the possibility of you being wrong is slightly more likely than you being right.

Friend: All things being equal.

Me: But as you say, we keep disagreeing. On *A, B, C, D, E…* How do you account then for the fact that, despite having a better than fifty-fifty chance of being wrong on each occasion, you are never wrong?

Friend: Like I say, it's because you're a pratt.

Me: A pratt with the same basic facts, intelligence and general education as yourself.

Friend: The trouble with you is you're a professional contrarian.

Me: Professional? If only.

Friend: Let's just say you disagree for the sake of disagreement.

Me: You mean I'm a compulsive liar?

Friend: Oh no, I'm not saying that.

Me: Yes, you are. You're saying I say things not because I believe them to be true, but just for the sake of disagreeing.

Friend: Let's just say you have the sort of personality that thrives on disagreeing.

Me: And you have the sort of personality that thrives on conforming?

Friend: Not at all, I disagree whenever I feel it is justified.

Me: Same here.

Me: Blah blah blah
Friend: You're bullshitting.
Me: No, it's what I happen to believe.
Friend: Well, I don't believe it.
Me: That's down to you.
Friend: I don't believe it because it's so outlandish.
Me: We disagree, is all.
Friend: But you come over like a bullshitter.
Me: I do, don't I?
Friend: You admit you're a bullshitter then?
Me: Not at all. Outlandish theories are advanced by bullshitters so I'm always conscious that when I advance my theories—which I accept sound outlandish—people are going to assume I'm bullshitting. If I try to compensate for that, I only manage to end up sounding like a bullshitter because that's what bullshitters are doing. Coming the other way, as it were.
Friend: Poor you.
Me: You're right, I'm no good at it. Bullshitters get away with it because they're experienced bullshitters. They've honed the technique over the years so they get believed. Or at any rate disagreed with on a good faith basis. Not being a bullshitter I never get the practice. So I don't get believed and nor do I get disagreed with on a good faith basis. I just get accused of being a bullshitter.
Friend: Poor you.
Me: Poor world.

Friend: Why do you have to be an arsehole all the time?
Me: It comes with the territory.
Friend: You mean all applied epistemologists are arseholes?
Me: Like I say...
Friend: It's not because only arseholes become applied epistemologists?
Me: You've got a point there but, no, not officially.
Friend: You've got a rule, have you, 'Thou shalt not be an arsehole'?
Me: We've got a rule 'Thou shalt disagree with people on fundamentals'.
Friend: What's that got to do with the price of fish?
Me: Whenever anyone finds themselves disagreeing with someone over fundamentals, they think that person is an arsehole.
Friend: Stupid people might think that.
Me: You just did.

Friend: So this applied epistemology generates new theories, does it?
Me: No, it disposes of old ones.
Friend: Sounds thoroughly negative.
Me: You have to remove a bad theory before you can come up with a better one. Applied epistemologists can be trained to recognise bad theories, there's no guarantee they'll be able to come up with better ones.
Friend: So mostly negative?
Me: Even if it was entirely negative it would still be a force for good. We live in a culture where 'Don't know' is not permitted so you have to clear a space before you can even get started.
Friend: A sort of philosophical flush toilet?
Me: If you like, but remember a flush toilet doesn't flush everything away.
Friend: Mine does. Except occasionally. Embarrassingly.
Me: But what does it leave behind? Every time.
Friend: Give up.
Me: It leaves fresh, clean water.
Friend: More a replacement, surely?
Me: Fair point. But you didn't consider that, did you? Despite a prompt from me. We only deal with things staring you in the face but can't see.
Friend: I feel tricked.
Me: I know. Applied epistemology often has that effect.
Friend: All right, now you've made me notice it, amaze me with your flush toilet insights.
Me: Invented in the sixteenth century and not improved on since. Worth thinking about.
Friend: I'll leave that one to someone else.
Me: You've been leaving it to someone else your whole life.
Friend: But applied epistemologists don't, is that the gist?
Me: Pretty much.

Me: I don't accept moral justifications.
Friend: More fool you. They are fundamental.
Me: They are only used when people have run out of arguments.
Friend: You do talk some tripe.
Me: Would you accept a justification 'God wills it'?
Friend: Of course not. That's not the same thing at all.
Me: Appeals to morality are of the same nature. Designed to end the argument.
Friend: So I'm not allowed to use, say 'fairness' as a benchmark?
Me: Only if you are arguing with people who think *un*fairness is something to be pursued.
Friend: Lots of people do. Fat cat billionaires do it all the time.
Me: No, they accept unfairness might result from policies pursued for other reasons.
Friend: *Will* result.
Me: You'll have to argue it out with them whether the 'other reasons' outweigh the unfair consequences you're so worried about.
Friend: They'll inevitably say they do.
Me: You'll inevitably say they don't. But fairness itself won't come into it. Unless you're losing the argument.

Friend: You've never lost an argument?
Me: Not a serious one, no.
Friend: What a mighty man you must be.
Me: I am, but it doesn't follow. Most people would be hard-pressed to remember losing a serious argument. It would have meant changing something serious in their brain. They would remember that.
Friend: But you're always saying people should lose fifty per cent of their arguments. Doesn't that apply to you?
Me: Presumably. But I don't get to have many because I'm always in the company of people who don't like serious arguments.
Friend: But you're always sounding off about something or other.
Me: Not 'something or other'. Something I know about. Something I'm bound to win.
Friend: How can you be sure of that?
Me: I'll be the only person in the room interested in whatever it is.
Friend: And soon the only person in the room.

Me and My Enemies

Academic: The trouble with people like you is that you wade into something and start throwing your weight around when you don't have any formal grounding in the subject.
Me: That's very true, though I'm surprised to hear you say I have any weight to throw around.
Academic: People like you cause us endless trouble, with your stupid conspiracy theories and sundry nonsense.
Me: How do know they're nonsense? Academics never read my stuff, for instance, and that isn't nonsense. Wrong-headed maybe, but not nonsense.
Academic: If they were any good, they'd be 'in the literature'.
Me: How? No peer-reviewed journal would accept anything by me, they're not written in academese.
Academic: Then write them in academese. As you call it.
Me: Not just me. When was the last time you came across any attack on the basics of your subject 'in the literature'?
Academic: I haven't, personally.
Me: Doesn't that disturb you?
Academic: Not in the least. We've been around since the nineteenth century. We've had all the time in the world to get the basics right.
Me: It's true they were laid down in the nineteenth century.

Academic: I'm not a fan of your style of revisionism.

Me: What style of revisionism are you a fan of?

Academic: How do you mean?

Me: For example, do you disagree with your colleagues?

Academic: Of course, all the time.

Me: You're a revisionist then. You wish to revise what they believe.

Academic: That's far too simplistic.

Me: I'm a simple soul, could you explain it to me?

Academic: I write a scholarly paper, it goes out for peer review, various people make comments, I *revise* the paper.

Academic: Thank you for your critique of my book. However, you seem to be taking issue with everything ever written on the subject.

Me: Only the bits I disagree with. Page seventeen, for instance, why do you believe that statement?

Academic: It's in any standard work on the subject.

Me: So?

Academic: It comes with a citation.

Me: So?

Academic: That means it was made by an accredited authority.

Me: Did he have a citation when he made it?

Academic: How could he? He was the originator of the statement.

Me: He made it up, you mean.

Academic: He came to a conclusion based on the evidence before him.

Me: You've checked that evidence?

Academic: I could if I wanted to.

Me: But you haven't.

Academic: Why would I? He's the accredited authority, far more conversant with the relevant evidence than I am.

Me: *Was.* I understand he lived in the Victorian era.

Academic: This book you've sent me. There seems to be no sources provided for many of the statements you make. Why is that?
Me: Because they are my own. I am the source.
Academic: Do you think I'm going to take seriously a book by an author who just makes things up as he goes along?

Academic: Your book lacks citations, it's worthless.

Me: It's full of citations. It's nothing but quotes from standard sources and commentaries on them.

Academic: But you don't give the source so they are worthless.

Me: But you accept they are standard sources of some kind?

Academic: No, why should I?

Me: It says so in the book.

Academic: Why should I believe that?

Me: You can always google a few words of one of them to check. If any of them fail the test, you are free to chuck the book in the bin.

Academic: I'm not going to do that. Nobody is likely to do that.

Me: I agree, but if anybody did, I will be speedily exposed as a charlatan, so it's not very likely I would, is it?

Academic: The thought did cross my mind.

Me: Do you check the citations in academic books?

Academic: No, I have no reason to. I can take them at face value.

Me: So you accept the validity of citations in books that are unlikely to be checked but not in a book where they might very well be.

Academic: This is all irrelevant anyway. I'm not going to bother with a cut'n'paste book that sticks to standard sources.

Me: What about a book that argues fundamental errors are best found in standard sources?

Academic: I'm certainly not going to bother with a book that claims anything so preposterous.

Academic: Why haven't you named any of the sources you use in your book, together with a bibliography?
Me: They are all standard sources.
Academic: So why not name them?
Me: Would you read a book with a citation bibliography that read Wikipedia, Wikipedia, Wikipedia, Encyclopedia Britannica, Wikipedia, Wikipedia, British Museum website, Wikipedia, Wikipedia…?
Academic: No.
Me: Would you read a book purporting to demonstrate that paradigm errors in academic subjects are best discovered in general textbooks, encyclopaedias, official websites and so forth, rather than in specialist academic papers?
Academic: That would be one of your books, I take it?
Me: Yes. You're perfectly safe, nobody reads them.

Academic: You spend so long hanging out with crazies you've become one yourself.
Me: You spend so long hanging out with academics you've become one yourself.
Academic: Don't be facile. Right or wrong, academics have at least gone through a certain number of rationality gatekeepers.
Me: You all go through the *same* ones, you all end up saying the same thing. A recipe for rationality, that's true, but not a good way of deciding what's right or wrong.
Academic: I'd prefer to call it 'checks and balances' but I'm not prepared to go down that road again with you.
Me: Fair enough, but you'd have to concede it is not exactly a recipe for radical thinking.
Academic: Thank God for that, from what I see on the internet.
Me: You don't believe in supping with the Devil, no matter how long the spoon?
Academic: No, I do not.
Me: I don't believe in devils. Or anything else supernatural.

Academic: You write the most extraordinary garbage.

Me: I always have a justification for why I have written it though.

Academic: No doubt that will be garbage too.

Me: That is unlikely.

Academic: Why? It will be a case of 'garbage in/garbage out'.

Me: You mean 'garbage out/garbage in'.

Academic: I know what I mean.

Me: I accept what I have written may be garbage, it is my own so it would be hard for me to judge. But the *reason* I've written it isn't my own, it will be a flaw I have spotted in a standard source.

Academic: Flaws that no-one else has spotted.

Me: Do you know anyone who examines standard sources for errors?

Academic: No.

Me: Have you ever spotted one yourself?

Academic: No.

Me: But you agree someone should do it, even if they can't find any?

Academic: No.

Academic: Take page three. You've got that wrong for a start.

Me: How do you know?

Academic: You can look it up in any textbook.

Me: I did.

Academic: So why are you saying the opposite?

Me: I disagreed with the textbook.

Academic: Mr Expert, are you?

Me: Well yes, in the sense I was writing a book on the subject.

Academic: You're right and the world's wrong, is that it?

Me: In this case, in my opinion, yes.

Academic: And you want me to agree with you on your say-so?

Me: I want you to agree with me for the reasons advanced in the book.

Academic: You think I've got time to read every cockamamie book that gets sent to me?

In the Pub

Me: Who's gonna win the title?
Bloke in pub: Liverpool.
Me: Which team do you support?
Bloke in pub: Liverpool.
Me: Which team will improve their position most?
Different bloke in pub: Manchester United.
Me: Which team do you support?
Different bloke in pub: Manchester United.
Me: Which teams will be relegated?
Other blokes in pub: The ones promoted from the Championship.
Me: Which teams do you support?
Other blokes in pub: Not ones promoted from the Championship.

Wiseacre: You picked those examples very carefully.
Me: I did, didn't I? I wanted to be more trenchant but was surprised at how rational football fans are in practice.
Wiseacre: Why do you suppose that is?
Me: Presumably because actual outcomes in football are precise, observable and constantly reiterated.
Wiseacre: Not something that applies in life generally.

Bloke in pub: What a load of old bollocks.

Me: Now that *is* interesting.

Bloke in pub: What is?

Me: I've just presented you with a complex idea, completely new to you, yet you were able to reject it in a matter of seconds.

Bloke in pub: So?

Me: That can only mean one of three possibilities.

Bloke in pub: What, other than you talking complete bollocks?

Me: No, that is one of the possibilities. The problem though with that explanation is it would mean you, a randomly selected individual, can instantly see something's complete bollocks, whereas me—having worked on it for years—can't see it at all. That would make me the dumbest person of all time.

Bloke in pub: Out of the mouths of babes, babe.

Me: But there's a *second* possibility. You have such a remarkable brain you can understand, process and reject complex and unfamiliar ideas in seconds. That would make me an ordinary joe and you the smartest person of all time.

Bloke in pub: I'm guessing it will turn out to be the third possibility.

Me: You are an ordinary joe behaving in the usual way when confronted with any new and complex idea. The human brain has to deal with this situation constantly so, if it had to judge each one of them on its merits, it would soon be snowed under. Hence, it has to reject all of them because it cannot know ahead of time which of them is worthy of consideration.

Bloke in pub: What a load of old bollocks.

Bloke in pub: What a load of old bollocks.

Me: Now that *is* interesting.

Bloke in pub: What is?

Me: You have just been presented with some alternatives of a complex nature about something that is completely new to you, yet you were able to reject all of them in a matter of seconds. That can only mean one of three things. Either the choices presented to you were so bad anybody could see they were absurd without breaking sweat. Apart from me. Ergo, I am the dumbest person of all time. Or*:* you have such a remarkable brain you could tell the alternatives were absurd in seconds even though an ordinary person, in this case me, thought they were perfectly reasonable. Ergo, you are the smartest person of all time. Or*:* you are an ordinary person behaving in the usual way when presented with novel but complex choices, you rejected them reflexively.

Bloke in pub: Ergo, it's my round.

Me: Same again, please. In a straight glass if you wouldn't mind.

Bloke in pub: That's just your opinion.

Me: Whose opinion were you expecting?

Bloke in pub: No, I mean who are you to say?

Me: M J Harper. My mum sewed it on my underpants.

Bloke in pub: No, I mean why should I listen to you?

Me: In the first place, you weren't listening.

Bloke in pub: I was, honest.

Me: In the second place, the opinion you hold was just someone's opinion when it started out.

Bloke in pub: But it's been through the mill since.

Me: In the third place, it's the one everyone holds and that's the only reason you hold it.

Bloke in pub: I'd be a fool not to by the sound of it.

Me: In the fourth place, it's an opinion that has been around forever only because everyone holds it, not because it's true.

Bloke in pub: Stood the test of time, I reckon.

Me: In the fifth place it was unsubstantiated when it was first thought up and has proved to be only a so-so guide since.

Bloke in pub: Better than nothing.

Me: In the sixth place, knowledge has moved on apace since it started out, so it's probably worth revisiting.

Bloke in pub: They probably are, as we speak.

Me: No, they're not. I know, I've made it my job to find out.

Bloke in pub: Well paid, is it, this job?

Me: No, everyone keeps saying it's just my opinion.

Bloke in pub: I'm glad to meet you in person at last after reading your books.
Me: I'm always glad to meet people who like my books.
Bloke in pub: What kind of people are they?
Me: They tend to talk about their own stuff for a bit and then we go our separate ways.
Bloke in pub: That's good because I was hoping to run a few of my ideas past you.

Me: I'm the happiest person I know.

Bloke in pub: Tell me about it.

Me: I thought everyone thought that about themselves.

Bloke in pub: Not me.

Me: What's the problem?

Bloke in pub: I'm Danish.

Me: I thought the Danes were supposed to be the happiest people in the world.

Bloke in pub: We are. We come top in surveys, year after year.

Me: So what's your problem?

Bloke in pub: I'm the happiest person I know, just like you. Only, unlike you, the people I know are Danes.

Me: I still don't see the problem.

Bloke in pub: If the Danes are the happiest people in the world and I'm happier than they are, I have some claims to being the happiest person in the world.

Me: And that's a problem?

Bloke in pub: Have you any idea what the pressure is like, having to be the happiest person in the world?

On the Sofa

Liberal British TV anchor: Both FBI and police data show crime is declining in Washington so why is President Trump sending in the National Guard?
Trump-supporting American: It worked in the LA riots.
Me (to television)**:** Why are you using such an absurd comparison?
Anchor: The crime numbers were already declining.
Trump-supporter: Declining from an unacceptably high level.
Anchor: In the last year: homicide down 12%, sexual abuse down 50%, robbery down 28%...
Me (to television)**:** These figures are so astonishing they should be the subject of the discussion.
Trump-supporter: They are still unacceptably high.
Anchor: But hardly the emergency President Trump is using to justify his action.
Liberal studio guest: Declaring an emergency was a technique used by Hitler in Germany and Mussolini in Italy.
Me (to television)**:** Why are you making this absurd comparison?
Trump-supporter: Trump is Hitler? Why can't he just be making a policy decision you disagree with? The comparison is comical.
Liberal: I hope and pray you're right and it's a ridiculous comparison.
Me (to television)**:** So why did you make it?
Liberal: History doesn't repeat itself but it rhymes. I fear Trump will turn America into an authoritarian state.
Me (to television)**:** In four years?

Me (later, to self)**:** Hitler managed.

Companion: These Russian incursions by planes and drones are very worrying.
Me: Not really, they're just provocations.
Companion: That makes them all right, does it?
Me: It means they are not incursions, they're provocations.
Companion: What's the difference?
Me: An incursion is something you have to deal with.
Companion: And provocations aren't, I suppose.
Me: Not if you want the provocation to be a successful Russian ploy.
Companion: So the Russians will just carry on doing it, won't they?
Me: Probably. For a bit. Then they'll try something else, their provocation policy having failed.

Companion: I don't agree with you about Ukraine, bullies should always be stood up to.

Me: Bullies should never be stood up to.

Companion: Why ever not?

Me: You'll get beaten up if you do.

Companion: What should you do then?

Me: Either pay up or run away.

Companion: Bullies will be everywhere if that policy is adopted.

Me: Bullies *are* everywhere. Wherever there is no effective law and order.

Companion: So combine and fight back.

Me: That would be providing effective law and order. It never happens.

Companion: Appeal to higher authority.

Me: And get beaten up the next day?

Companion: What would you do? They're a real problem at Barnaby's school.

Me: Nothing.

Companion: Great!

Me: Bullies police themselves. There are always as many as the situation allows. That's why bullying is always a problem at school but never an intolerable problem.

Companion: So NATO is just another bully alongside Russia, is that it?

Me: Oh no, NATO is the ineffectual law-and-order. America is the other bully.

Me: You're suffering from a lack of self-esteem.
Companion: How do you know?
Me: It's part of the female condition.
Companion: You're an expert, are you, being a man?
Me: Just an expert on sex.
Companion: Not that I've noticed.
Me: I mean gender. Women congenitally suffer from low self-esteem.
Companion: Probably just the ones you know.
Me: Human beings are intelligent animals and since intelligence is genetically determined, both parents must be intelligent. But for intelligence to be effective, children have to be cared for over an inordinately long period of time. Which means in turn the whole family unit has to be supported for a long period of time.
Companion: You worked all that out on you own, did you?
Me: The two roles are completely different so the most efficient way to do this is to specialise, one role/one parent.
Companion: And who ordained it would have to be women that drew the short straw?
Me: Only women can suckle offspring, so it made evolutionary sense to give them the child-rearing role.
Companion: So when that role is finished they can go off and men can stay at home for a change.
Me: It doesn't finish though, does it? Not until you're both so old you both want to stay at home.
Companion: I think we would have spotted the flaw in that plan by now. We're intelligent, you said evolutionary biology ordained it.
Me: Exactly. So evolution made sure you had the 'chronic low self-esteem unless bringing up offspring' gene.
Companion: So how come I have to go out to work while you loll about the place?
Me: I need leisure time to work all these things out.

Out and About

Bus queue: [Long-suffering silence.]

Me (looking at bus arrival time stuck on 1 min)**:** It's the longest minute in human history.

Bus queue: [Stony silence.]

Me (brightly)**:** It's positively Einsteinian.

Man in queue: Do you know what a plank is?

Me: Are you calling me a plank?

Man in queue: Max Planck.

Me: Oh, him.

Man in queue: Yes, him. Do you know what a *planck* is?

Me: I used to.

Man in queue: It's the ten to the power of minus forty-three part of a second.

Me: I knew it was there or thereabouts.

Me: First time I've ever been in a hybrid.

Taxi driver: Second time you've been in this one.

Me: One would never know.

Taxi driver: Second time you've mentioned about it being a hybrid.

Me: Sorry, memory's not what it used to be.

Taxi driver: Down for the opening ceremony, are you?

Me: Yes, my mother's being presented to the Queen.

Taxi driver: They generally bus a few in from the care home.

Me: I really couldn't say.

Taxi driver: Met the Queen twice myself. Prince Phillip three… no, tell a lie… four times. Never Prince Charles for some reason. Royal protection squad… great days.

Me: I'm an applied epistemologist myself.

Taxi driver: [Yawn]

Me: I'm not boring you, am I?

Taxi driver: Sorry. Brighton wait-and-return last night. Didn't get a lot of kip.

Me: Ah, Brighton. Used to live there. Sally Thomsett's a good friend.

Taxi driver: Not familiar with the name.

Me: In *The Railway Children.*

Taxi driver: Laurence Olivier used to be one of my regulars. Nice chap.

Me: Not familiar with the name. By the way, your controller was a bit weird when I rang.

Taxi driver: You don't have to tell me.

Me: She thought Shepstone Manor was a village. Then she asked me for the postcode. How would I know the postcode? What a dummy.

Taxi driver: She's not from round here. Comes up from Weymouth to cover weekends.

Mick: Why would anyone use a controller who's not local?

Taxi driver: I bring her, she's my wife.

You: So what's this been all about, squire?

Me: Well, I was experimenting with the genre on my website, as a modern take on the Socratic Dialogue, to get some of my theories across.

You: Did it work?

Me: No, but I found people were sufficiently diverted to actually read them, something I have not always found to be the case with books, lectures and YouTubes where I put my theories forward.

You: And you think we're going to make a beeline for them now, is that it?

Me: That's it exactly but I know, wearing my professional hat, people either won't and it will be wasted effort on my part, or they will and it will be the worse for me.

You: May I take it your theories don't go down very well?

Me: You may. Though 'not going down very well' is a far cry from the spleen they seem to evoke in those that read enough to judge them.

You: I feel sorry for you, I really do.

Me: Really? And there I was feeling sorry for *you*!

You: Well, if that's the way you feel, you can fuck right off.

Printed in Dunstable, United Kingdom

75618187R00068